Get off *the* Pot and DO Something!

In Pursuit of MORE

Get off the Pot
and DO
Something!

Get off *the* Pot *and* DO Something!

In Pursuit *of* MORE

DOUGLAS SCOTT

Get off the Pot and DO Something

DOUGLAS SCOTT

I want to dedicate this book to my
wife Marcia who has been my greatest
source of loving encouragement.
Thanks, Darlin.'

Acknowledgments

I want to acknowledge my mom and dad and the many teachers who have encouraged me to pursue God for more. I also want to thank the many people who have been in the life groups I have taught as we have studied and walked this life journey together. A special thanks to Pastor Jaime Rodriguez for his wisdom, insight, encouragement and, most of all, his friendship. More, please!

Get Off the Pot and Do Something!
In Pursuit of More
© 2019 Douglas Scott
Published in Yorktown, Virginia, USA

This book or parts thereof may not be reproduced in any form, stored in a retrieval system, or transmitted in any form by any means—electronic, mechanical, photocopy, recording, or otherwise—without prior written permission of the publisher, except as provided by United States of America copyright law.

Scripture quotations marked NIV are taken from the Holy Bible, New International Version®, NIV®. Copyright © 1973, 1978, 1984, 2011 by Biblica, Inc.™ Used by permission of Zondervan. All rights reserved worldwide. www.zondervan.com. The "NIV" and "New International Version" are trademarks registered in the United States Patent and Trademark Office by Biblica, Inc.™

Scripture quotations marked NKJV are taken from the New King James Version®. Copyright © 1982 by Thomas Nelson. Used by permission. All rights reserved.

Library of Congress Control Number: 2020902522

International Standard Book Numbers:
Hardcover: 978-1-7342577-2-4
Trade paper: 978-1-7342577-0-0
E-book: 978-1-7342577-1-7

Printed in the United States of America

Table of Contents

Introduction xi

Chapter 1 Foundation 1

Chapter 2 Level 1 Maturity 5

Chapter 3 Setback 9

Chapter 4 Comeback and New Discovery 13

Chapter 5 Worship Was Key 21

Chapter 6 Outside Influences 25

Chapter 7 Application 43

Chapter 8 Marketplace Ministry—
Change the World? 49

About the Author 53

INTRODUCTION

THIS IS MY story, but I believe a lot of people are experiencing the same things that I went through. There are two groups of people. First, there are those who are stuck in a religious system that may have provided a good biblical foundation, but they are not experiencing the present-day power of God. There is even a commitment to spiritual disciplines like Bible reading, prayer, and church attendance. But the focus seems to be on maintaining what you have without a lot of thought of becoming a disciple or discipling other people. I heard someone put it this way: "I have the fire insurance, and now I just try not to mess up." Apostle Paul would have probably put it this way: "having a form of godliness, but no power."

Second, there are a group of believers who know that God has more, and they are passionate about seeing the realities of heaven demonstrated in the earth. You know, like Jesus said, "Kingdom of God come, will of God be done, on earth as in heaven." They are connecting with other believers at conferences and seminars. They are reading books, taking courses, watching DVD series, etc. to increase their knowledge and understanding.

But at some point, you have to "step out of the boat." It's time to do more than just learn. It's time to put all that knowledge into action. It's time for us to create safe environments where people are allowed to "practice" and not be criticized. No one does a new thing right the very first time. You have to begin. Trust God. Take a chance.

This book is my story from my perspective. I will say this a few times in this book: "you don't know what you don't know." That is a real challenge that can only be met by passionately pursuing God and looking for people who are further along than you are in seeing heaven demonstrated on earth. Notice I didn't say people who were older than you were. I have met many younger people who were far more successful in doing the work of the ministry than I was. But my passion gets stirred, and I'm determined to be a God Chaser all my life!

Chapter 1

FOUNDATION

I HAVE A SIGN hanging in our home that says, "Home is where your story begins." My story began in 1949 in a little town in southern Indiana called Seymour. Seymour is in the south-central part of Indiana about sixty miles south Indianapolis and about sixty miles north of Louisville, Kentucky. Seymour was surrounded by a lot of farming and was basically a farming community with a few factories, one of which was Arvin Industries where my dad worked. The population of Seymour in the 1960s was about 12,000 people. Our graduating class in 1968 had about 280 students. Seymour is often referred to as the crossroads of Southern Indiana. The Pennsylvania Railroad and the B&O Railroad intersected right in the center of town. Our family consisted of dad (Gayle Scott), mom (Geneva Scott), me (the oldest child), then Randy, Debbie, and Tim. Life was a lot different and a lot slower when I grew up. We had party line telephones and no televisions. Life was all about family and revolved around the church. Seymour, in those days, had what were known as the blue laws. Blue laws meant that no stores were allowed to open on Sunday—no service stations, no restaurants. There may have been one drug store (pharmacy, in today's terms) that was open for a short time to cover emergencies. Grocery stores that were within one block of a church were not allowed to sell alcoholic beverages or tobacco products. There were no shopping malls, and people shopped downtown. Life revolved around the church, and church was not only foundational to the family, it was foundational to the community. Schools recognized the importance of church and did not schedule activities on Wednesday, because that was church night. In those days, school began with a bible verse, prayer, and the pledge to the flag. Consequently, growing up we had a strong biblical foundation. In the 1950s and 1960s, about 70 percent of the people had a strong belief in God versus today; that percentage is less than 51 percent. Over half of the population made church a regular part of their life. Whereas today less than 27 percent of people would say that their life revolved around church.

I grew up attending Seymour First Church of the Nazarene. Our church and the First Baptist church were the two largest churches in town that I recall. There were, of course, various other churches from denominations such as Methodist, Pentecostal Holiness, Church of God, Presbyterian, Catholic, Lutheran, and more. Most churches had church on Sunday morning, Sunday night, and Wednesday night. It was also pretty standard to have a two-week revival in the spring and in the fall. Amazingly, we never missed a service and always managed to get our homework done and strived for perfect attendance in school.

There were so many people that cared and shared life

together. We were a part of a real community of believers that imparted Godly wisdom and understanding in lots of us young kids. Ray Worman was a farmer who had the biggest hands, but he loved fifth grade boys and taught our Sunday School class. There was Wilma Gossman who taught our Bible Quiz team, and, even today, I am so thankful for the Bible that was instilled in me through countless hours of study and quizzing. All of us kids were on her bible quiz teams at one time or another. There were three older ladies who taught our senior high Sunday School classes: Erma Hill, Liz McClain, and Edna Audis. These ladies didn't feel like they had to become teenagers to be able to teach us. They were godly and respected teachers who genuinely loved us to Jesus. Besides, our dads would have taken us to the proverbial woodshed had we misbehaved. Mom and Dad were key people in the church, and of course in my life because the bible was not only taught, it was lived out at home. I know my backside received the rod of correction, usually Dad's belt, when words were not enough to get the point across. Mom and Dad were youth leaders, as well as Sunday School teachers. Dad served on the church board as long as I can remember, and he took care of a lot of the maintenance issues at church. Dad could fix just about anything, which I guess came in part from being a maintenance foreman at Arvin Industries. Many Sundays I had the treat of riding with Dad on the church bus to go pick up kids who didn't have a way to church. Mom and Dad were always serving, and that part of life was instilled in us kids at an early age. My brother Randy retired from the Marine Corp and moved to Texas where he served on the board at his church. He and Edana (his wife and granddaughter of Edna Audis) are involved in children's ministry teaching Sunday School. My sister Debbie retired from teaching school and has always worked with children. Debbie and her husband, Steve, are also involved on the worship team in their church. My youngest brother Tim just retired from Crane Naval Weapons Station and has served on the board at his church and has been the district bible quiz director. Tim and his wife, Vicki, have carried on the tradition of teaching kids the bible through bible quizzing. So, you can see that the foundational truth of God's word was instilled in us kids at an early age and has born a lot of fruit and continues to produce to this very day. I am forever grateful for Christian parents and a community of believers that invested in kids and helped develop within us a strong biblical foundation. For us, going to church was not an option. It was life. When the doors opened, we were there—Sunday morning, Sunday night, Wednesday night, and every night if there was a revival going on. Giving was not an option. From the very first allowance, Dad taught us that the tithe belonged to God and came out first. Bible reading and prayer were not just options, they were vital for maintaining a right relationship with God and growing to be a good disciple of Jesus. The foundational biblical truths that were not just taught but lived out every day were absolutely vital in establishing the character and wisdom that has carried me through life. We developed a heart for serving, giving, and sharing the love of Jesus whether it was at church or at our job.

Chapter 2

LEVEL 1 MATURITY

AFTER HIGH SCHOOL I was off to college at Purdue University where I studied electrical engineering for four years, and upon graduation, I moved from Seymour Indiana to Newport News, Virginia. The pastor that we had growing up in Seymour was Dr. B. G. Wiggs. He was very good friends with a couple who lived in Newport News, Virginia, where I was moving to go work for Newport News Shipbuilding. So, traveling halfway across the country, I started my search for Wayne and Abby Kendall. Wayne worked for the C&O Railroad, and when I found them, I was invited to spend a few days with them while I was waiting on my mobile home to be delivered to Newport News, Virginia. Obviously one of the first things that I wanted to do was find a church. Since I grew up in the Nazarene church, I joined Wayne and Abby Kendall who were members of the Hampton Church of the Nazarene. Now that I had graduated and had begun the next phase of my life and career, I wanted to get involved in ministry. This was a natural thing for me because it had been demonstrated to me all of my life. I started out working with the college and career class at the church. This began what I thought was a natural maturing process of not only teaching the college and career class but working with the younger youth as well. I was soon appointed as the youth leader for Hampton Church of the Nazarene and served on the church board. I also was involved in teaching the children in children's church. The things that I learned when I was in high school and growing up, all the Bible quizzing, all the Scripture memorization, and all the Bible stories gave me a wealth of knowledge and experience to speak into the lives of these young people.

I had a pretty strong background in music. Mom and Dad wanted all of us kids to learn how to play the piano, and I was in band from the sixth grade all the way through graduation at Purdue University. I became involved in the choir at the Nazarene church, and, in addition to teaching and being involved in church administration, I eventually became the worship leader and choir director for the Hampton Church of the Nazarene. The Nazarene church had what today would be called a traditional worship service which was similar to what I had grown up with in Indiana. In other words, it was pretty much hymn based. This was also about the time that new choruses began to emerge from companies like Maranatha Music and Hosanna Integrity. We were beginning to use overhead transparencies and to project the words of the choruses on the screen and move a little bit away from holding hymnals to a more contemporary worship service. So again, using the talents that had been imparted and cultivated in me as I grew up, I began to work with the choir to do Easter productions and Christmas productions. I was maturing and expanding in the things that I had seen demonstrated as a child. To me that was the natural maturing process that you go through in being a disciple, i.e., you reproduce the things that have been reproduced in you. I was involved in teaching. I was involved in leadership. I served on the church board. I was involved at a district level in judging teen talent contests. I was fully involved in many areas of ministry that were going on at the church using the gifts and talents that I believe God had given me.

Chapter 3

SETBACK

AFTER BEING AT the Hampton Church of the Nazarene for probably eight to ten years, I had the misfortune of going through a divorce. At that particular time in history and even somewhat today, it was like reading/living *The Scarlet Letter* by Nathaniel Hawthorne. Now I carried this stigma/symbol around because I had been divorced. My life had been damaged. I was eventually replaced as music director and had to step aside from most of the ministries that I was involved in. It got to the point that I could not effectively serve the church. I couldn't be involved in leadership and all the things that for eight to ten years that I had invested in and worked in. All of the ministries that I was growing in and maturing in pretty much come to a screeching halt. Because of the divorce situation, the church considered that I was not suited to be part of leadership and I was no longer suited to lead worship. As a result of all of the rejection I felt, I left the Hampton Church of the Nazarene very discouraged, very hurt, and feeling pretty much worthless. I felt that my life and my involvement in the church ministry was pretty much over. Honestly, I had been treated better by some of my friends at work who didn't go to church than some people who went to church.

I remembered that Wayne Kendall and I had gone to a revival at a church called Warwick Assembly of God. Wayne had made the comment to me that if he ever went to another church it would be Warwick Assembly of God. Since I found myself needing to move to a different church, I said, "Well, I'm going to try out Warwick Assembly of God". I started attending Warwick and learned that they had a class for singles. Several of them in the class had been divorced, and they were interested in restoration and healing. They didn't look down upon me. They didn't criticize me. They just loved me and spoke into my life. During this Sunday School time, our teachers, Charlie and Sandy Forbes, just poured into all of us hurting wounded people who had been through tragic life situations. You see, Charlie and Sandy had been through the same situation that several of us had been through. But instead of being rejected, they were able to provide a time of healing and restoration for hurting people. We were just trying to recover and trying to make sense of everything that was happening to us. There was an expression several years ago that Christians are the only ones who shoot their own wounded. Warwick was truly a place of restoration and healing. God's love was demonstrated without any condemnation or judgmental spirit.

During this time, I developed a relationship with a lovely lady named Marcia. Marcia had been divorced as well and was part of Charlie and Sandy's class. Marcia was a very outgoing person and was instrumental in my restoration. I am somewhat the opposite from Marcia and it would have been easy for me to withdraw and sit in the corner licking my wounds. Marcia has never met a stranger and consequently, as I "tagged along" with her, I met a lot of new people and began to get involved where I could. Eventually, Marcia and I got married, and she has been my biggest supporter. She has been a true Barnabas and has encouraged me in every area of my pursuit for more of God.

Chapter 4

COMEBACK AND NEW DISCOVERY

THE COMEBACK

IT SEEMED LIKE a natural instinct that I needed to be involved somewhere doing something in the church. I had always heard that we were not saved to sit but saved to serve. I would never be satisfied just sitting on the sidelines. Gerald Frix was leading the choir and the worship band at Warwick Assembly. He asked me if I would like to play in the band. Wow! I had played trombone since I was in the sixth grade and continued in the band and orchestra at Purdue University. This was a great opportunity, and I was happy that I would be able to use my talents for God again. I began to play in the band for worship. I also began to sing in the choir and be involved in the Christmas and Easter productions that the church produced. I heard there was an opening to teach the College and Career class. Slowly I began to again use the foundational things that I had learned and began to teach a College and Career class. God had begun the restoring process. God began to heal the hurt and renew me from the inside out. I taught those young people and college-age kids and marveled at what God was doing in so many of their lives. I look back at the fruit that came out of those classes and saw guys who became pastors, missionaries, worship leaders, and Sunday School teachers. God was showing me that He was a God of restoration. Romans 8:1 says, "There is therefore now no condemnation to those who are in Christ Jesus, who do not walk according to the flesh, but according to the Spirit" (NKJV). God doesn't condone our bad choices; He is a God of reconciliation. There is life after divorce. I became pretty involved again and was teaching a Sunday School class. I was involved in music and worship. But there was just this "thing" that was hanging out there. It was like the enemy said, "Well, you can do all these things, but you will never be involved in leadership again." Being part of the leadership team was one of the things I really thrived on. Being involved with leadership and helping to discover how we would fulfill God's vision for the church was really important to me. After being involved at Warwick Assembly of God for several years, there was an opening on the church board for the secretary of the board. The guy who had been secretary was not going to return and serve on the board. Pastor Cheshire asked me if I would allow my name to run as secretary of the board. I said, "Sure, if that's all right with you. I would love to do that." At the annual business meeting, I was elected as the secretary of the church board. Boy, my heart was just leaping for joy, and I was celebrating on the inside. It was almost too much to believe. When I walked out in the parking lot it was like

God spoke to me, not in an audible voice, but in my spirit. God said, "Now you see, I can restore everything that the enemy has taken away." I could hardly contain myself. The joy of the Lord erupted all over me.

NEW DISCOVERY

Stepping aside for the moment, I want to take a look at what I saw the differences were between the Church of the Nazarene and the Assemblies of God. My intention is not to knock or try to discredit either denomination. I am very thankful for my Christian heritage and the love for the Bible and God that was instilled in me from my earliest years of recollection. I'm looking at this in retrospect and recognizing that at the time, I felt like I was growing and maturing as a Christian was supposed to. I felt that I was on a discipleship track, in that I was being a disciple, I was learning, I was growing, and I was maturing in ministry. The things I had gotten fulfillment from, such as teaching, music, and leadership, were maturing and growing. These things were my goals and the things I would strive to improve. So, looking back at the denominations, the Nazarene church would be classified as Wesley Armenian in their doctrine and would be considered a holiness denomination. The Nazarene church believes that there are two definite works of grace. First, there was the salvation experience of being saved by grace through faith in Jesus Christ. Secondly, there is a subsequent work of grace that is referred to as "entire sanctification" which was being filled with the Holy Spirit, also referred to as the baptism of the Holy Spirit. The Nazarene doctrine is somewhat cessationist. I was taught that some of the things that happened to believers, as mentioned in the book of Acts, only happened on the Day of Pentecost or during the time of the disciples, such as "speaking in tongues." I was taught that the "miracle" of speaking in tongues was that everyone "heard in their own language" and not that everyone spoke in an unknown language. In any case, it was primarily for the initial spreading of the gospel and not for today. Also, the gifts Christ gave to the church (Ephesians 4:12–13) that seemed to be pertinent for today were the Evangelist, Pastor, and Teacher. The gift of Apostles was only the original twelve, minus Judas plus Paul. The gift of prophecy was not discussed. As far as the gifts of the Holy Spirit mentioned in 1 Corinthians 12 and 14, I was pretty much taught that all were acknowledged for today except the tongues and interpretation of tongues. Tongues was considered "unnecessary" unless maybe you were a missionary and God gave you a gift of a specific language for a specific people. There was no mention of a prayer language or heavenly language. We were taught that the Spirit interceded with groanings that could not be uttered and therefore there was no language, just the Holy Spirit groaning. So, this cessationist doctrine basically said that a part of the working of the Holy Spirit ended with Jesus or at least ended when the last apostle died.

The Assemblies of God was classed as a Pentecostal full Gospel Church. Which, according to my initial observation, meant they spoke in tongues. The Assemblies of God believe that you are saved by grace through faith, just as the Nazarenes believed. The Assemblies also believe in the subsequent baptism of the Holy Spirit, the only difference being, they believe that the initial evidence of the baptism of the Holy Spirit is speaking in tongues. They believe in the present day working of the gifts of the Holy Spirit including tongues and interpretation of tongues.

I also didn't hear mention of apostles or prophets as gifts to the church. It seemed to me initially that the Assemblies were full Gospel to the point that they spoke in tongues where the Nazarene church didn't. So, neither denomination seemed to teach all five of the gifts Christ gave to the church which are referred to as the fivefold ministry of the church. Ephesians 4:11–13 says that the gifts are "to equip his people for works of service, so that the body of Christ may be built up until we all reach unity in the faith and in the knowledge of the Son of God and become mature, attaining to the whole measure of the fullness of Christ" (NIV). The purpose of the gifts was for the maturing of the church so that we would become Christ-like and we would do the things that Christ did. Jesus, when He sent out His twelve disciples, as recorded in Matthew 10:7–8, said, "As you go, proclaim this message: 'The kingdom of heaven has come near.' Heal the sick, raise the dead, cleanse those who have leprosy, drive out demons. Freely you have received; freely give" (NIV). The lifestyle of the present-day disciple of Christ should be preaching the gospel of the kingdom, healing the sick, raising the dead, cleansing the lepers and driving out demonic spirits because we have freely received and we should freely give away.

When I look at either one of the places where I was growing and maturing, we believed in healing and saw healing. Even I have been healed on at least two different occasions. But we didn't see a whole lot of the signs and wonders and miracles. I mean, I've never seen a person raised from the dead. I've never seen anybody cleansed from leprosy. I have seen demonic spirits cast out of people. It seems like our present-day ministry is pretty much preaching, teaching, and evangelism, but there is not a whole lot on the signs and wonders that are supposed to follow believers. Paul stated on one occasion that he didn't come with fancy words of men's wisdom, but with the demonstration of the Spirit's power. How is the power of the Spirit present? I heard someone say that we can sing our three fast songs, our three slow songs, take an offering, and give an analysis of a scripture, and we don't need the Spirit's power. Sure, there were people being saved. There were people being healed, but it was somewhat on a limited basis. I began to hear of the power of the God being demonstrated overseas, but why not in America? If it was happening overseas, then it was a present day working and not just something that happened at the time of the disciples. So, how "full gospel" were we really?

As recorded in Acts 2:4, all of them were filled with the Holy Spirit, and they began to speak in other tongues as the Spirit enabled them. Peter got up and began to address the crowd because they were speculating that the disciples and the 120 that were in the upper room had been drinking and were drunk. However, Peter, when he began to address the crowd, he repeated a prophecy that was spoken by the prophet Joel which says, "In the last days, God says, I will pour out my Spirit on all people. Your sons and daughters will prophesy, your young men will see visions, your old men will dream dreams. Even on my servants, both men and women, I will pour out my

Comeback and New Discovery

Spirit in those days, and they will prophesy. I will show wonders in the heavens above and signs on the earth below, blood and fire and billows of smoke. The sun will be turned to darkness and the moon to blood before the coming of the great and glorious day of the Lord" (Acts 2:17–20, NIV). Peter's giving an accounting of what was supposed to happen. What was prophesied by the prophet Joel (that in the last days when the Spirit was poured out) obviously happened. Joel prophesied that when the Spirit was poured out, your sons and daughters would prophesy. This was another thing that I didn't see being taught in either of the denominations. There was no teaching about prophecy and the gift of prophecy. There was no teaching on what it meant to be a prophet and what New Testament prophecy was all about. There was no teaching about seeing visions and dreams and understanding that God talks to us in dreams and visions. There was no teaching on dream and vision interpretation.

Most of the modern denominations began in the fire of an outpouring of the Holy Spirit. Overtime, due to any number of reasons, there became a lack of the demonstration of the Spirit's power, and doctrines began to be watered down and explained away as cessationism or not even relevant at all for our time. So, the challenge is how do you know what you're missing out on? How do you find out what you don't know? Because, *you don't know what you don't know!*

Chapter 5

WORSHIP WAS KEY

THE ASSEMBLIES OF GOD had a freer form of worship. It wasn't just singing hymns, which is good. We began to sing scripture songs. The Bible admonishes us to sing psalms, hymns, and spiritual songs. We sang psalms and hymns, but what were these spiritual songs? I soon discovered that at the end of some of the choruses, we didn't rush to the next song, but we began to tarry and sing spontaneous songs from our heart. Sometimes these songs were in English and other times they were in "tongues." Even though the words of this spontaneous song may not have been understood, there was an inner refreshing as the Spirit began to sing through us. I had a deeper and deeper passion for this intimate worship. I would go to various events, such as the "Catch the Fire" conferences with John and Carol Arnott that were sponsored by the Christian Broadcasting Network (CBN). This opened up a whole new avenue of accessing Spirit-filled worship and seeing signs and wonders and miracles. God was creating a greater hunger within me for His presence, and I knew there was a whole lot more than what I had been seeing. I attended a Leadership Conference at Grace

Church in Franklin, Tennessee that was sponsored by John Arnott. Again, I was introduced to wonderful musicians who had a heart for spontaneous worship. Their humility and passionate pursuit of the Spirit were contagious. Kimberly and Alberto Rivera were some of the passionate spontaneous worshipers to whom I was introduced. The hunger for more of God's presence was growing. I was also introduced to a church in Redding, California that was pastored by Bill Johnson where they said there were hundreds of miracles that were being documented.

Another local church, Bethel Temple Assembly of God began a revival with evangelist John Davis who had been part of the outpouring in Pensacola, Florida, known as the Brownsville Revival. I had gone to Bethel Temple because of a bad attitude. John Davis preached a sermon entitled, "Is there a doctor in the house?" At the end of the service during the altar call, John said "and God can heal you of a bad attitude." I knew God had found me, and I repented. I was hungry to hear more from God, and I returned the next night, which happened to be Thanksgiving Day. One of my friends was on the worship team, and I told him I would like to be part of their team when my church was not having services. He introduced me to worship leader Scott Smith. Scott introduced me to the worship band, and I began to play with them on Thursday, Friday, and Saturday evenings while still attending Warwick Assembly on Sunday and Wednesday. I was seeing God move in greater ways, and the hunger for deeper, more intimate worship was stirring within me. Scott Smith introduced me to the International Worship Institute led by Lamar Boschman. I ended up attending the

International Worship Institute for about ten years. I was again introduced to deeper and more passionate worship. It was more than just singing songs, but true worship for who God is. I was introduced to songwriters like Darlene Zschech, David Baroni, Matt Redman, and many others. I was introduced to musicians like Alvin Paris and Tyrone Williams who were great instrumentalists who had such a humility and passion for God's presence that was contagious. I was introduced to Vivian Hibbert who taught about prophetic worship. I learned how to prophesy on an instrument. How to play over people prophetically and see the power of God released in their lives. This opened up whole new areas to which I had not been exposed. Looking back again, this emphasized—*You don't know what you don't know*

At one of the International Institutes, we were introduced to Mike Bickle, who leads the International House of Prayer (IHOPKC) in Kansas City. They had started 24-hour prayer led by worship teams. This was another new concept that I had never explored. Again, it was passionate spontaneous worship that was more than just singing songs but communing with God and adoring His presence. Misty Edwards was one of the worship team leaders. Her passionate spontaneous worship was so contagious that everyone wanted to sing these heart songs of adoration to Jesus. There was so much more of a closeness when we moved away from written words and began to sing from our heart. At this time, IHOPKC has been going nonstop for more than twenty years.

Worship and pursuing a closer more intimate relationship with God caused me to look everywhere I could to find people who were moving with the Spirit of God in ways that the New Testament described. I was hungry for more! *You don't know what you don't know*, and it's extremely important to pursue God wherever He leads, even if it means stepping and learning from people outside of your denomination. After all, denominations were not God's idea. They have created a lot of separation in the body of Christ. That doesn't mean we accept bad doctrine, but we should focus a lot more on what we agree on and work out the rest.

Chapter 6

OUTSIDE INFLUENCES

THERE HAVE BEEN a lot of outside influences. Some of them I have referred to. But what seems to be a common thread is passionate worship and a heart to see God move like He did through Jesus and the early disciples. A spark ignites when we hear stories of how God is moving, and we begin to pursue God for more. We must look for places where there are greater expressions of God's presence and begin to pursue with greater passion for more of God. We tend to get in ruts doing good things and miss out on doing the greater things for the Kingdom. Below are some of the outside influences that have sparked a greater passion for more of God's presence in me.

JOHN AND CAROL ARNOTT—
TORONTO AIRPORT CHRISTIAN CENTER

Like I said earlier, I was introduced to John and Carol Arnott at a Catch The Fire conference at CBN in Virginia Beach, Virginia. I saw "fire tunnels" where people were getting radically touched and people were getting healed.

One night the cameras videoed a person who had one of their teeth turn to gold. I went to an International Leadership Conference in Franklin, Tennessee. John taught about the Father Heart of God. He taught that God was good. God was not angry. He was compassionate and desired a closer relationship with us more than we did. We met two of his associates, Alan and AJ Jones. They taught us a four-line prayer and began to give testimony after testimony how God had used that prayer to heal people. Here's the prayer:

> *This healing belongs to me*
> *Because of what Jesus has done*
> *I receive my healing now*
> *In Jesus's name.*

I have used this four-line prayer many times and seen people healed. It's not that I was looking for a formula, but there are two parts to every prayer: the giver and the receiver. Jesus freely gives, but too many times people do not receive. It's important for people to exercise their faith and let God demonstrate what He has done. A young man named Kenny came to me at church one Wednesday night and said his Nana had told him to come find me and have me pray for his shoulder. It was about ten minutes before church was supposed to start, and I was trying to find a fuse for the sound system. I said, "Why don't you wait until after church, and I'll pray for you"? He said, "No, you have to do it now. Nana said you would." So, I led Kenny in the four-line prayer, and he repeated it after me. After we finished, I said, "OK, do something you couldn't do." He looked kind of puzzled and began to slowly lift his arm over his head. He began to do jumping jacks, and I joined in. The Pastor happened to walk out of the side door and asked, "What are you guys doing?" I said, "Kenny has just been healed." Later on, in the service, Kenny was lifting his son over his head with both arms in the air. Praise God! While at Grace Church I heard another testimony from a church in Redding, California that really grabbed my spirit as I begin to realize that God wants to be actively involved in our everyday lives. Somehow, we have settled into a survival mode in lieu of taking the offensive and actually being the disciples Jesus called us to be.

BILL JOHNSON—BETHEL CHURCH IN REDDING, CALIFORNIA

At Grace Church they played a testimony of a person being healed on "aisle 5 in Walmart"—I think that was the story. Bill Johnson is part of a revival network with John and Carol Arnott and several others. I was hearing about how God was moving at Bethel Church in ways that I wanted to see. They were seeing things that seemed to have been relegated to Jesus when He was on earth and to His disciples. One key phrase was—Kingdom of God come! Will of God be done! On earth as in heaven! I was hearing about the realities of heaven becoming the realities on the earth. The gospel was being demonstrated with power that I had only heard about. The first Bill Johnson book I read was *The Supernatural Power of a Transformed Mind*. An insatiable appetite began to grow in me for more of what God was doing. I was no longer satisfied with just "trying to stay out of trouble," I wanted to be a real disciple. One of the key verses that I have highlighted in my Bible is Matthew 10:7–8 where Jesus is sending out His disciples with this commission which says,

> As you go, proclaim this message: 'The kingdom of heaven has come near.' Heal the sick, raise the dead, cleanse those who have leprosy, drive out demons. Freely you have received; freely give. (NIV)

I began to really believe that God's intention was for the realities of heaven to become the realities in the earth. Some people might argue that what Jesus said in Matthew was just for His disciples. But if you look at other passages, such as Luke 10, there were seventy-two that were sent out to declare that the kingdom of heaven was at hand and to heal the sick. They came back to Jesus, declaring in Luke 10:17, that even the demons were subject to them in Jesus's name.

I heard that Bethel Church was documenting the miracles that were taking place because they wanted to be sure that God was getting the glory. My spirit was being stirred. I began to download the podcast from Bethel, and my daily commute to work consisted of listening to the Bethel podcasts over and over until they became a part of me. I began to share with others the insights I was receiving and how I was being challenged to press in deeper to what God was really calling His church to do. I have made several trips to Redding and also through the podcasts was introduced to Kris Vallotton, associate pastor at Bethel and head of their School of Supernatural Ministry.

KRIS VALLOTTON—ASSOCIATE PASTOR AT BETHEL CHURCH IN REDDING, CALIFORNIA

On the Bethel podcasts, I heard stories about the School of Supernatural Ministry and how the students were sent out on mission trips to various places around the world. The students came back with reports of healings and various other miracles. Kris taught about prophecy and emphasized Acts 2:17–18 where Peter declared that Joel 2:28–29 had been and was being fulfilled.

> In the last days, God says,
>   I will pour out my Spirit on all people.
> Your sons and daughters will prophesy,
>   your young men will see visions,
>   your old men will dream dreams.
> Even on my servants, both men and women,
>   I will pour out my Spirit in those days,
>   and they will prophesy. (NIV)

I don't know how many times I had read over those verses and never thought about being one of the sons that was supposed to prophecy and that God actually talked to us today through dreams and visions. I guess I had always looked at prophecy from an Old Testament perspective and not the New Testament perspective. You see, New Testament prophecy can be foretelling, but it seems to be more "forthtelling." The Apostle Paul says in 1 Corinthians 14:1 that we should "eagerly desire gifts of the Spirit, especially prophecy" (NIV). Then Paul says in 1 Corinthians 14:3:

> But the one who prophesies speaks to people for their strengthening, encouraging and comfort. (NIV)

Again, I was being stretched way beyond what I had been taught. I learned that Kris hosts the School of the Prophets and teaches about Basic Training for Prophetic Activation. I have been to this school two different times and have not only received information, but also received practical application and training in what was being taught.

Here's an example of what I'm talking about. I was working at Newport News Shipbuilding in Newport News, Virginia. My office building was at a remote location from the shipyard and in a not so good neighborhood. There had been several shootings, and numerous times bullets had been found in our parking lot. I was a security representative for my building so I was always on the lookout for people walking the streets that might enter our parking lot. My main responsibilities were to provide computer support for the Submarine Engineering Division. Frequently I would have to go to the main part of the shipyard and pick up computer passwords for new people or for people who needed their password reset. On one occasion, as I was driving to the main shipyard, I saw a lady walking up the street. I "felt like" God said to pull over and give her some money. Well, it's very rare that I would just give people money because my thought is that they will buy cigarettes or booze and just waste money. I would rather buy food or something like that so the money is not wasted and contributing to a bad lifestyle. So, I kind of started this conversation with myself. "That's probably not God, because

I don't give money to people walking the streets." I was stopped in traffic at the intersection of Marshall Avenue and 39th street waiting for the light to change and then the woman was walking on the sidewalk past my truck. Again, I heard this "still small voice" say, "You need to give this woman some money." Again, I said to myself, "I don't just give people money, however, if I see her when I return, I'll give her some money." There was a small grocery store on the other side of the intersection, and I figured that that was where she was going. I also guessed that I probably wouldn't see her again, so I was free from the voice or thought that I should give her some money. I continued toward the main part of the shipyard and picked up the password for the employee. I was coming across the 39th Street bridge and had to stop at that same intersection at 39th and Marshall Avenue. Amazingly, that same woman was walking across the street in front of the waiting traffic. Now what should I do? Well, I turned the corner, and the thought came into my mind, "I can't stop and get to her. She is on the wrong side of the street." I continued a little farther and started to turn into the parking lot of the building where I work. I looked in the rearview mirror, and I saw the lady had crossed to the other side of the street and was heading down a side street. Now I'm thinking I could certainly go down the side street. So, I stopped wrestling, turned the truck around, and headed down the side street. Meanwhile Proverbs 3:5–6 had been going through my head.

> Trust in the LORD with all your heart
> and lean not on your own understanding;

> in all your ways acknowledge Him,
> and He will direct your paths. (NKJV)

I pulled over just a little ahead of where the lady was and got out of my truck. I walked up to her and said, "Good morning, I believe that God has highlighted you to me and wants me to give you some money. I don't have much money. All I have is twenty dollars, but I want to give it to you. And I believe God wants to say to you that if you 'Trust in the LORD with all your heart and lean not on your own understanding; in all your ways acknowledge Him, and He will direct your paths.' God wants you to know that He knows where you are, and He is looking after you. Just trust Him."

She gave me a big hug and thanked me. I got back in my truck and started back toward my building. On my way back, God reminded me that I had awakened at exactly 4:35 AM three days in a row. I thought, *Well, maybe God is trying to tell me something.* When I got back to my desk, I got out my Bible and randomly opened to what would have been the New Testament. I did that a couple of times and didn't open up to a book that had 35 verses in chapter 4. I said to myself, *Maybe the verse is in Psalms.* Psalm 4 only had eight verses. I then randomly opened further back in the Old Testament and opened to Deuteronomy. I'm thinking, *Well, the odds of finding something here will be pretty slim.* I turned to chapter 4 and there were thirty-five verses.

> You were shown these things so that you might
> know that the LORD is God; besides Him there
> is no other. (NIV)

My eyes flooded with tears, and I knew God had been talking to me. I just needed a little more boldness to step out and trust Him for direction. I have learned that even if you were to miss what God was saying, you can always give a person a word of encouragement.

Kris has also written a book called *Spirit Wars*. To me this was another area that was not being taught. Kris was so transparent in exploring situations that he had been in and had encountered. There are many people who are being oppressed by the enemy, and it's important to be able to deal with these situations. A lot of times we don't realize that the underlying issue is a spiritual issue and not a physical or mental issue. The root of some illnesses is a spiritual issue, and it manifests itself by affecting us physically. For example, some cases of arthritis are actually related to unforgiveness and bitterness. To be healed from some physical issues requires that the spiritual issue needs to be dealt with first.

JOHN PAUL JACKSON— STREAMS MINISTRIES

Another person that I was introduced to through Bethel Church was John Paul Jackson. John Paul was probably the leading person in the country on biblical dream interpretation. Sadly, John Paul Jackson passed away in 2015. Again, this was an area about which I had never heard taught. If God is really speaking to us in dreams, how many times have we missed out on what God was telling us? I have a teaching from Jeannine Rodriguez, who was mentored by John Paul Jackson, where she says "an uninterpreted dream is like a letter that is never opened." Wow—to think of the years of dreams that have never been interpreted.

I took two online courses from Streams Ministries—"The Art of Hearing God's Voice" and "Understanding Dreams and Visions." Dreams are basically "nighttime parables." While some dreams are literal, the majority of our dreams are metaphors or parables, similar to the parables that Jesus taught. Also, look at the dreams that Joseph and Daniel had that were told about in the Old Testament. They were symbolic, not literal. Secular dream interpretation will not give you the correct interpretation of your dreams. The Holy Spirit is the one who provides the answer. When Daniel was called to interpret the dream that Nebuchadnezzar had, he responded in Daniel 2:27–28a:

> Daniel replied, "No wise man, enchanter, magician or diviner can explain to the king the mystery he has asked about, but there is a God in heaven who reveals mysteries." (NIV)

Every dream that is recorded in the Bible was externally received. It was not internally generated. Therefore, the Holy Spirit provides the meaning, not our own psyche.

Again as we quoted earlier from Acts 2, if we are living in the last days, if the Holy Spirit has been poured out, if we are being given dreams and visions, shouldn't we be teaching people how to seek the Holy Spirit for the interpretation rather than saying, "that must have just been some bad pizza?"

Here is one of the dreams I had:

Outside Influences

I was in our family room, and I got up from the couch and looked underneath the couch. I saw that a large section of carpet had been cut out. When I looked up, there was a large conference room table turned sideways in the family room. On the other side of the room I saw a person on stilts, like a sheetrock person would wear. I began to gesture and move toward the person to make them nervous and cause them to fall. I didn't want to touch the person, just make them nervous and fall on their own. Then I woke up.

I have learned that when I have dreams like this, God is trying to tell me something. I began to ask the Holy Spirit for the interpretation. I felt the Holy Spirit gave me the following interpretation. The couch represented something I was comfortable with. The missing carpet was a flaw that was hidden in what I was comfortable with. The conference room table represented a business organization. The person on the stilts represented someone who had become unstable, i.e. they were in a position where they could easily fall. Here's the application, and it applied to my job. The old director (old organization) that I was comfortable with was being replaced by a new director (new organization). There was a person in the old organization who had a flaw that was hidden from normal view. I wanted to expose the person making them unstable and causing them to fall. In this dream, God was showing me that I needed to take my hands off the situation and leave the outcome up to Him. It was not up to me to make the person unstable and cause them to fall. This was a warning dream from God that I needed to leave my work situation up to Him. I am so thankful that I had learned to listen to what God was saying in my dreams.

Mark Virkler—Founder and Director of Communion with God Ministries and Christian Leadership University

Mark developed a course called "The Four Keys for Hearing God's Voice." Mark developed this course out of his own journey to discover what God's voice sounds like. Many people say, "God told me to do something," but very few people are able to say what God's voice sounds like or how they knew it was God speaking to them. I will tell you what the four keys are, however, this listing of the keys will not be sufficient for you to learn how to hear God's voice. It is necessary to study these keys, see the biblical references, discuss how we are made as humans and practice listening. Most of us get so busy running here and there that we don't take time to listen. So, here are the four keys:

1. Quiet yourself down.

2. Fix your eyes on Jesus.

3. Tune to spontaneity.

4. Journal.

First of all, most people don't get quiet long enough for God to speak to them. We are the busiest people on the planet, running in every direction and seldom stopping. Secondly, our eyes and our minds are running fifty different directions, and it's hard to focus on a single thing for any period of time. We wait for a few seconds, and then we are running off to the next thing. If you want to hear from Jesus, you need to focus on Jesus. Thirdly, tune to spontaneity. You'll have to take Mark's course to have a good understanding about spontaneity, and it will take some practice to get somewhat proficient at hearing the spontaneous things God is speaking. The fourth step is very key, and that is journaling. It's important to write down what God is saying. First off, it shows God that you really care and value what He is saying to you. Secondly, it helps you remember what God is saying to you. It's important to remember what God is saying. It may take some practice to get good at journaling. One of Mark's quotes is, "People say that anything worth doing is worth doing well." However, "no one does something new very well for the first time." So, it will take time and practice to get proficient at journaling, but it is well worth the effort. Practice taking notes when your pastor is preaching. After all, we all believe that God speaks to us through our pastor's message. So why not take notes.

In June of 2018, Marcia and I had the privilege of going to Israel with a group from church. I journaled almost every day that we were there. The most special day for journaling was the day we went to the Garden of Gethsemane. What better place to "quiet yourself down, fix your eyes on Jesus, tune to spontaneity, and journal". I was sitting on the ground leaning back against an olive tree. I could just picture me and Jesus taking a break and resting against the tree. The following is my very personal journal entry.

Me: Not my will but Your will be done! I surrender to Your plan and Your purposes for my life.

Me: What would You say to me?

Jesus: I see your heart. I see how you pursue Me. I see the things that concern you and Marcia. I will give you strength.

Me: Lord, I need You to be more and more real to me. I need Your strength. I need Your answers. I need You.

I need You more
More than words can say
I need You more
I need You more
You are the air I breathe
You are the song I sing
You are my everything
My heart's desire
I need You more
I love You, Lord
I worship You

Me: In the midst of the clamor (horns were blowing in the background), You are my peace.

Me: I'm asking for Marcia's healing. Give her a new heart—perfect rhythm, perfect valves.

Jesus: My perfect plan is unfolding. Trust Me, and I'll bring you through. Don't lose patience. The race is not to the swift, but to the one who endures.

You are a champion of the cross.
Victorious!
You will fulfill your destiny.
You are fully equipped to do what I have
called you to do.
Be strengthened! Be at rest!
I've got you covered. My favor surrounds you
like a shield!
Be strong in the power of My might.
Do great exploits for the Kingdom. WE ARE
MORE THAN ENOUGH!
Be strong and of good courage
The battle is Mine says the Lord
The victory is already won.
It is manifesting at this very moment!
The joy of the Lord is your strength.

Needless to say, my eyes were so full of tears I could hardly see to write. My heart was overwhelmed!

On one other night while we were in Jerusalem, several of us had taken the metro to the old part of the city. On the way, someone noticed a grand piano sitting on the street in front of city hall. One of the ladies encouraged me to play the piano. As I began to playing spontaneously from my heart the music shifted to the song "Let it rain! Let it rain! Open the floodgates of heaven! Let it rain!" In my spirit I began to say, "God, let Your Spirit rain down on

Jerusalem." The next Saturday as we were walking though the old part of the city of Jerusalem, it began to sprinkle rain. Later that day one of the guys in the group said our tour guide said it hadn't rained in Jerusalem in June for about eleven to twelve years. We took that as a sign that God was going to pour out His Spirit in a greater measure over Jerusalem.

It's amazing how much more we hear from God when we just quiet ourselves down and focus on what He is saying!

Kevin Dedmon—Author of The Ultimate Treasure Hunt

The subtitle to Kevin's book is "A Guide to Supernatural Evangelism Through Supernatural Encounters." I was introduced to Kevin's teaching and his book through Bethel Church in Redding, California. Again, I was hearing about the miracles and the supernatural encounters that people were having at Bill Johnson's church. There was a hunger stirring inside of me for more of what God was doing. Kevin was leading people on "spiritual scavenger hunts" to find people that God was highlighting to his team. These were people that God wanted to supernaturally encounter. In the introduction to his book Kevin writes,

> "*The Ultimate Treasure Hunt* is about supernatural encounters. It is about learning to live a naturally supernatural Kingdom lifestyle, in which miracles, physical healing, the prophetic and setting people free are normal occurrences,

as we release the presence and power of the Kingdom of God to the people we know and meet every day."

Kevin tells about setting down with a team of three or four people and praying and waiting on God believing that God wants to encounter people with the realities of heaven. Some people might call it "soaking" or quieting yourself down and focusing on Jesus. Sounds familiar, huh? The team began to write down things that they believed God was highlighting, like the color of clothing, places, ailments—anything that might be unique. Then the team got together and shared what they believed were clues to who God was leading them to encounter. And then the hunt began. It is amazing the number of people that have been encountered.

On one of our "treasure hunts" there was a group of us at the local mall preparing for a Christmas musical presentation. We had some time to spare, and I said, "Why don't we go on a treasure hunt because surely there is someone here at the mall that God wants to touch? We quieted ourselves down and began to pray and ask God who He would highlight that we could minister to. One person had the word "Games." Someone else had the clue "green shirt." Someone else had the clue "personal tragedy." There were several other clues, so we each took our sheets and the clues the team had and began to walk through the mall. We came across a "GameStop" store and said maybe this is the place God is leading us to. We entered the store, and one of the sales associates had on a green shirt. Two of us approached the sales person and began a conversation. After a short while, we explained that we believed God may have pointed him out to us. We showed him some of the clues that we had. We asked him if there had been a traumatic event in his life. He said that his best friend had just committed suicide. We shared that we believe that God had sent us to him to reassure him and comfort him. To let him know that God knew what he had been through and was there for him every minute of the day. We were able to encourage him and share the love of God with him.

Encounters like these are what really get us pumped up about what God is doing and what God wants to do. The opportunities are endless, and God is waiting for people like us to make ourselves available for Him to use. Many of us for years have just walked past people with no thought about who God might be wanting to touch through us. It makes a difference when we begin to see the marvelous things that God is doing and wants to do through people who are hungry for more of God.

Chapter 7

APPLICATION

IT'S VERY IMPORTANT that we pass along the information we have learned. Like I said in the beginning, we don't know what we don't know. It's easy to get settled in our day to day life and get into survival mode in lieu of thrive mode. We must remember that there are thousands of people out there who are in the same situation that we were in. Maybe there is a lack of hunger. Maybe there is false theology. There are any number of reasons why we are not looking for more. Tommy Tenny wrote a book called *God Chasers* that many people are not pursuing the "more" of God. God is able to do exceedingly abundantly above all we could ask or think, but are we allowing God to use us to stir a hunger in the hearts of people for more? We have to pass along the information that we have learned not just in a classroom setting, but also in a marketplace setting. One of the best ways to pass along what we have learned is by practical example. It means a lot more to see something demonstrated than to just hear about it in a classroom setting.

Next, we not only have to pass along what we have learned, we have to help others apply what we have learned and what they are learning. Applying what we have learned seals the idea or new teaching in our hearts. It's like teaching someone a new computer skill. You can explain what the keystrokes are, and you can show them the results of what you are doing, but the application is cemented in their mind when they are pressing the keys and they are executing the commands. Personally, applying what we have learned pushes us to the next step in what God is teaching us. There is always more when it comes to God and how He is moving and leading us.

We must help others realize that there is more to our Christian experience than just maintaining what we already have. Like I mentioned earlier, sometimes we get into survival mode and forget that we are supposed to be talking about the Kingdom, healing the sick, raising the dead, casting out demons, and cleansing those who are unclean. We live in a very me-oriented society, and we have to change that attitude. Jesus said we are the greatest when we are serving others. So, life is more than just maintaining until Jesus comes, it's helping and encouraging others and helping to develop them to the point that they are discipling others.

God has called us to be fishers of men, not keepers of the giant aquariums. Our churches should be places of celebration about what God is doing in the marketplace. One of our church slogans was "we are a church without walls." Many churches have become very me-focused and forget that we have been commissioned to go into all the world, beginning at home first and then going out from there.

I have taught classes for many years, but more recently, I believe I have actually equipped people to do the work of

Application

the ministry. I have put together a five-part teaching series using the information and training that I have received from many "outside" sources. I call it the "Equip Series".

Equip 101:
How to Hear God's Voice

- This course in the foundational class in the Equip Series.
- In this class you will learn what God's voice sounds like.
- You will learn techniques that will help you focus on what God is saying.
- You will be able to tell others what it means to hear God's voice and how to distinguish between God's voice and other voices.
- This course uses a video series that was developed by Mark Virkler.

Equip 102:
Understanding Dreams and Visions

- Prerequisite: Equip 101
- Acts 2:17 says that when the Spirit is poured, our young men will see visions and our old men will dream dreams. God is speaking to us, but are we listening?
- In this course you will learn the various types of dreams.

- You will be able to distinguish between God given dreams and "bad pizza."
- Dreams are "nighttime parables." You will learn how God uses symbolism to speak into our lives.
- How many times has someone told you a "crazy dream"? Maybe God was talking? Maybe the "skinny cows were eating the fat cows"? Did you miss an opportunity to share what God might be trying to speak to a person?
- This course uses video material from Mark Virkler, John Paul Jackson, and others

Equip 103:
Basic Training for Prophetic Ministry

- Prerequisite: Equip 101
- Acts 2:17 states that when the Spirit is poured out, your sons and daughters SHALL Prophesy.
- Do we understand what New Testament prophesy is?
- Do we understand what "words of knowledge" are?
- This course material was developed by Kris Vallotton, an associate pastor for Bill Johnson and the head of the School of Supernatural Ministry at Bethel Church in Redding,

California. Kris also heads the School of the Prophets Conference at Bethel Church.

Equip 104:
Spirit Wars

- Prerequisite: Equip 101
- We wrestle not against flesh and blood, but against principalities and powers, against the rulers of darkness, against spiritual hosts of wickedness in heavenly places... This course exposes the devices of the enemy and is a practical resource for dealing with spiritual battles. This course gets to the root causes of some of life's issues that can only be dealt with by confronting the enemy.
- This course material was developed by Kris Vallotton, an associate pastor for Bill Johnson and the head of School of Supernatural Ministry at Bethel Church in Redding, California. His book *Spirit Wars* deals with issues that he has been exposed to and walked through victoriously.

Equip 105:
The Ultimate Treasure Hunt

- Prerequisite: Equip 101 and Equip 103
- This course is a practical guide to doing the work of the ministry. This course is certainly not the only way but is a way to be involved

in releasing God's goodness that brings transformation into people's lives. At the end of this class, students will be involved in Spirit directed "treasure hunts" to find people (treasure) that God wants to speak to. This is not only practical but a fun way to see how the Holy Spirit will direct you to speak His word to people in need.

Chapter 8

MARKETPLACE MINISTRY— CHANGE THE WORLD?

WE ARE LIVING in the information age where there is so much information that we have a hard time deciding what to spend our time on. We can Google search about anything and get more information than we could possibly use. I believe the key to maturing spiritually is finding people who are ahead of you in a certain area and see what they are doing. Like I have mentioned many times, you don't know what you don't know. We get so excited about learning more and seeing more that we sometimes get stuck running from seminar to conference to events and we don't take time to put into practice what we are learning. We can reach information overload and get stuck not knowing what to do with what we have learned and seen. We get caught up chasing "good" things and forget that we must get off the proverbial pot and put this learning into practice. Thus, the title I believe God gave me for this book.

The first part is pursuing God with everything that is in us. We need to see where He is moving and what He is doing. Once we see where people are doing things that we have not yet experienced, we have to measure that against what the Bible says and learn where we may have fallen short. We have to see where we may have latched on to some bad doctrine or where we have settled for something like a "cessationist lie" instead of a full pursuit of what is possible with God. Then we learn, we experiment or maybe I should say "test" the new learning to make sure it is of God and where God is leading us. It seems a little scary sometimes to try a new thing, but it's better to try and fail than to have never tried at all. God is gracious, and He is interested in our success as we pursue Him. God is good, and anything that denies that is a lie. God's very nature is His goodness. We have hope that God is good and will respond to our needs as we seek Him. I like Bill Johnson's definition of hope: "hope is the joyful anticipation of the release of God's goodness." Our hope is not wishful thinking. It's the anticipation that God is good, He is a good Father, and He will not withhold any good gift. God has commissioned us to "re-present" Jesus and talk about the kingdom of heaven. But not just talk, we must demonstrate the kingdom of heaven. God wants the whole world to know about His redemption plan. So, He is equipping us and empowering us to fulfill the Great Commission.

Jesus said, "I only do what I see the Father doing, and I only say what I hear the Father say." We are called to a deeper relationship, so we are hearing better and seeing better than we have before. But like Apostle Paul, we must do more than talk about the gospel. The gospel must be demonstrated with the power of the Holy Spirit. It's time to stop doing and start being the church. Marketplaces are where the hurting people are. It was the marketplaces where Jesus touched people in their everyday lives.

There is always more, and there will always be people who are ahead of us in various areas. Some of those people may be outside of our denominational stream. We must seek God wherever He is moving. We must mentor our younger generations and help them in areas that we have had to learn. We must mentor by example and not just in word. God convicted me in that I have learned a whole lot more than I have applied.

I hope this book inspires you to pursue God with all your heart. Learn that there is always more, and never lose the hunger to see what God is doing, even if it's outside your denomination. Judge what you learn against the Word of God. God will never violate the principles of His Word. And as God reminded me, "Get off the pot and do something."

Paul said in Ephesians 4, that our training and learning was "to equip his people for works of service, so that the body of Christ may be built up until we all reach unity in the faith and in the knowledge of the Son of God and become mature, attaining to the whole measure of the fullness of Christ" (Ephesians 4:12–13 (NIV). You see, our learning is not just to obtain more information but to enable us to do "works of service." We are to be an instrument that God can use to build the kingdom. Also note that this equipping is to bring us to the "whole measure of the fullness of Christ." In other words, until we are walking like Jesus walked, talking like Jesus talked, and doing what Jesus did, we have more to learn and experience. And by the way, *You don't know what you don't know!*

PS. I'm not saying that I have not put into practice the things that I have learned. Where I felt convicted by the Holy Spirit was that I have learned a whole lot more than I am practicing in my day-to-day life. While I have practiced the things I have talked about, they need to be much more of a part of my everyday life. It's not just learning and doing, but it's about integrating what you have learned into your day-to-day routines. It's walking consciously aware that there are people you pass each day that need to hear about a Jesus who loves them. Sometimes it just takes a scripture that releases God's word into their life. Sometimes God will move miraculously to get a person's attention. However, all signs point to Jesus. Every person deserves an encounter with Jesus, and you just might be the one to introduce them to Jesus.

Be a God chaser, and never stop pursuing more of God!

About the Author

DOUGLAS SCOTT IS a graduate of Purdue University (BSEE) and Old Dominion University (MEM). He recently retired as a Master Shipbuilder after 45½ years at Newport News Shipbuilding. He serves as a Life Group leader and serves on the leadership team of his local church. He is a lifetime learner and disciple searching for more of what God is doing and desiring to equip the body of Christ. He has attended various conferences and schools such as the International Worship Institute, Change the World School of Prayer, School of the Prophets at Bethel Church in Redding, CA, and the International Leaders Conference with John Arnott. He has a Certificate of Biblical Studies from the Potomac School of Ministry and is completing his Certificate of Ministerial Leadership from the Potomac School of Ministry.

Notes

Notes

Notes

Notes

Notes

Notes

Notes

www.ingramcontent.com/pod-product-compliance
Lightning Source LLC
Chambersburg PA
CBHW011801090426
42811CB00007B/1006